Sports Illustrated KIDS

Traditions and Superstitions

BASEBALL'S
Best
TRADITIONS
and WEIRDEST
SUPERSTITIONS

by Elliott Smith

CAPSTONE PRESS
a capstone imprint

Published by Capstone Press, an imprint of Capstone
1710 Roe Crest Drive, North Mankato, Minnesota 56003
capstonepub.com

SPORTS ILLUSTRATED KIDS is a trademark of ABG-SI LLC. Used with permission.

Library of Congress Cataloging-in-Publication Data
Names: Smith, Elliott, 1976– author.
Title: Baseball's best traditions and weirdest superstitions / by Elliott Smith.
Description: North Mankato, Minnesota : Capstone Press, [2023] | Series: Sports illustrated kids: traditions and superstitions | Includes bibliographical references and index. | Audience: Ages 8–11 | Audience: Grades 4–6 | Summary: "Going to a baseball game? Don't expect the teams to care about a rookie's first home run. But do watch for Bryce Harper's bat tapping ritual each time he's up for bat. But first, slide into the ins and outs of good fun and good luck in baseball. With engaging text and striking photos, this book will delight young sports fans with some of the best and weirdest practices on the field and in the stands"—Provided by publisher.
Identifiers: LCCN 2022005368 (print) | LCCN 2022005369 (ebook) |
ISBN 9781666346558 (hardcover) | ISBN 9781666346589 (pdf) |
ISBN 9781666346602 (kindle edition)
Subjects: LCSH: Baseball—Miscellanea—Juvenile literature. | Superstition—Juvenile literature.
Classification: LCC GV867.5 .S588 2023 (print) | LCC GV867.5 (ebook) | DDC 796.357—dc23
LC record available at https://lccn.loc.gov/2022005368
LC ebook record available at https://lccn.loc.gov/2022005369

Editorial Credits
Editor: Ericka Smith; Designer: Tracy Davies; Media Researcher: Svetlana Zhurkin; Production Specialist: Katy LaVigne

Image Credits
Alamy: Reuters/Danny Moloshok, 13, Reuters/Jessica Rinaldi, 19; Associated Press: 25, Eric Christian Smith, 17, Matt Slocum, 29, Steve Nesius, 7, Ted S. Warren, 11, Wilfredo Lee, 21; Getty Images: Focus on Sport, 15, Sports Illustrated/Herb Scharfman, 16; Library of Congress: Music Division, 14; The New York Public Library: 12; Newscom: Icon SMI/Allen Fredrickson, 27, Icon Sportswire/David J. Griffin, 28, Icon Sportswire/Nick Wosika, 10; Shutterstock: BearFotos (goat), cover, 5, Dan Thornberg (baseball), cover and throughout, DGIM studio (burst background), cover and throughout, Heike Brauer, cover (toothbrush), Hong Vo (licorice), cover, 24, mhatzapa, 18, Mott Jordan, cover (title fonts), mTaira, 5 (top), PotaeRin (fried chicken), cover, 22, zieusin, 8; Sports Illustrated: John Iacono, 9, Manny Millan, 23

All internet sites appearing in back matter were available and accurate when this book was sent to press.

Printed and bound in the USA. 4882

TABLE OF CONTENTS

Words in **bold** are in the glossary.

A LONG HISTORY

Baseball has a long history filled with traditions and superstitions. Some teams have been playing since the late 1800s. So some practices have been around for more than 100 years. Baseball is also hard. The best hitters make an out 7 out of 10 at-bats. So when players start doing well, they want to repeat the success. Before long, superstitions are born.

But whether they're simple gestures or **elaborate** routines, baseball's traditions and superstitions help make it a treasured experience for players and fans.

THE CURSE OF THE BILLY GOAT

Perhaps the most famous baseball curse happened to the Chicago Cubs. In 1945, William Sianis tried to attend Game 4 of the World Series at Wrigley Field—with his goat. When the goat was denied entry, Sianis was upset. He told the Cubs they'd lose the World Series that year—and that they'd never win the World Series again. The Cubs did lose the 1945 World Series. They didn't make it to the World Series again until 2016—but they won that year.

CHAPTER 1

IN-GAME TRADITIONS

The action on the field is just one part of what makes baseball fun. There are many **rituals** on and off the field that make the game exciting. Sometimes they're just as entertaining as the game.

DON'T STEP ON THE LINES!

A baseball diamond is marked with white lines called **foul lines**. They show what's **fair** and **foul** territory. As players go in and out of the dugout, many will jump or skip over the foul lines.

Why? Most players don't actually know. It's just something they've learned over the years. Some don't touch the lines out of respect for the grounds crew who drew them. But pitchers are often superstitious about foul lines. They believe that if they step on a foul line while heading back to the dugout, they will give up a run in the next inning.

Tyler Glasnow jumps over a foul line on his way to the pitcher's mound.

NEVER JINX A NO-HITTER!

A no-hitter is one of the most difficult **feats** in baseball. Through the 2021 season, there were only 314 in Major League Baseball (MLB) history. When a pitcher gets close to no-hitter territory, players, broadcasters, and fans start to watch their words. They all want to avoid **jinxing** the pitcher's chances.

Announcers won't mention there's a no-hitter in progress. Washington Nationals broadcaster Bob Carpenter will say a pitcher is "untouched."

During an attempted no-hitter, pitchers are the loneliest player on and off the field. No one talks to them to avoid distracting them. And most players won't even sit near the pitcher.

Nolan Ryan threw seven no-hitters during his MLB career—a league record.

HOME RUN FUN

Hitting a home run is one of the most exciting parts of a game. Players and teams have created all sorts of traditions around homers. Some teams have elaborate handshakes. Others use props. The Boston Red Sox use a laundry cart to give batters a ride. The Toronto Blue Jays give a home run hitter a jacket. It has the countries the players and staff call home.

The bat flip is a new way players celebrate a home run. They twirl their bats high in the air after connecting on a **long ball**.

When **rookies** hit their first home run, they are given the silent treatment. The player returns to a quiet dugout. The other players act like nothing happened. After a minute, they all begin to celebrate.

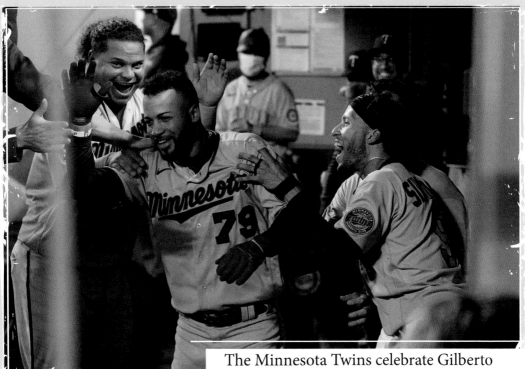

The Minnesota Twins celebrate Gilberto Celestino's first home run.

KANGAROO COURT

Keeping up with the official and unwritten rules of baseball can be hard, so teams often have a "kangaroo court." In the clubhouse, players pay fines for mistakes. But it's all in good fun, and the money usually goes to charity at the end of the season.

CHAPTER 2

FAN TRADITIONS

Not to be outdone by the players, fans have created their own traditions. Some are specific to certain teams and ballparks. Others are shared by fans across the country.

K IS FOR STRIKEOUT?

Fans write a backward *K* on their scorecards to note hitters struck out without swinging on their third strike. This type of bookkeeping has its origins in 1859. That year reporter Henry Chadwick began publishing **box scores**. Eventually Chadwick would use *K* for a strikeout.

Henry Chadwick

Chadwick had already used *S* for another play. He used *K* for a strikeout because *k* is the last letter in *struck*—a word used at the time for a strikeout. Writing the *K* backward has become a way to clear up whether a strikeout had a nonswinging final strike.

TAKE ME OUT TO THE BALL GAME

In 1908, songwriter Jack Norworth saw a sign while riding the subway in New York City. It said, "Baseball Today—Polo Grounds." He was inspired and wrote the lyrics to "Take Me Out to the Ball Game."

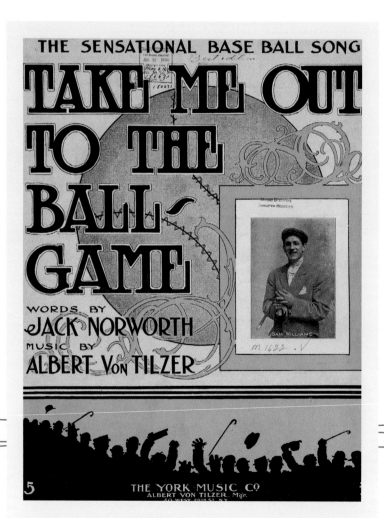

Norworth hadn't been to a game when he wrote the song. But his baseball song became a big hit. "Take Me Out to the Ball Game" was first played during the 1934 World Series. But the tradition of singing the song during the seventh-inning stretch—a break between the two halves of the seventh inning—didn't catch on until 1946. Since then, it has become a staple at ballparks all over the United States.

The Chicago Cubs made the song even more popular. Broadcaster Harry Caray would sing the song to the Cubs—a practice he actually started in 1976 when he was an announcer for the White Sox. Now Cubs fans join the sing-along during every home game.

Caray singing "Take Me Out to the Ball Game" at a Cubs game in 1989

THROW IT BACK!

As a fan, there's almost nothing worse than seeing your team give up a home run. But a small act of **defiance** has given fans some revenge—throwing the ball back onto the field.

Like many baseball traditions, throwing a home run ball back started in Chicago. In 1970, Atlanta's Hank Aaron hit a ball into the **bleachers** at Wrigley Field. A fan angrily threw it back onto the field. The tradition quickly spread across the country.

Hank Aaron at bat in a game against the Chicago Cubs in 1970

A Houston Astros fan throws a ball back during a 2019 game against the Seattle Mariners.

Now, fans try to throw the ball as far as they can. Sometimes the ball makes it all the way back to home plate! Some clever fans bring baseballs into the stadium. That way they can keep their home run souvenir and still throw a ball back.

SWEET CAROLINE

In 1997, a Red Sox employee decided to play "Sweet Caroline" at Fenway Park in honor of a friend who had recently had a baby and named her Caroline. Red Sox fans enjoyed singing along to the song. But it wasn't until 2002 that it became a tradition.

Now, before the bottom of the eighth inning, Neil Diamond's 1969 song starts up. Red Sox fans go wild and sing along. Diamond himself performed the song at Fenway Park in 2013.

"Sweet Caroline" is also considered the team's lucky song. The Red Sox have won four World Series championships since beginning the tradition.

Diamond sings "Sweet Caroline" at a Red Sox game in 2013.

CHAPTER 3
PLAYER SUPERSTITIONS

MLB players have worked hard to get to the big leagues. They've sharpened their skills and talents over many years. But when it comes to snagging a win, they rely on a little good luck too. Many players have rituals that help them win.

BRYCE HARPER GOES BATTY

Bryce Harper is one of the best hitters in baseball. He has hit at least 30 home runs in a season four times. He's also very superstitious. In 2013, he claimed to eat waffles before every game. He also said he took seven showers a day. It's all part of a routine he thinks helps him succeed.

But Harper's most noticeable superstition happens every time he steps into the batter's box. He does a complex tapping routine. He steps in the box and scrapes the dirt. He then taps each side of home plate. Next, he taps his big toe with the bat. Then, he lifts the bat up and looks at the pitcher. Now, he's ready to hit.

BUBBLE GUM LUCK

Yankees slugger Aaron Judge starts each game by putting two pieces of bubble gum in his mouth. He won't spit out the gum until he makes an out at the plate.

THE CHICKEN MAN

Third baseman Wade Boggs was known for two things. He was a great hitter. And he had some unique superstitions. Before every game, Boggs would eat a bucket of fried chicken. No one loves chicken that much, right? Boggs did.

Boggs was planning on writing a cookbook with his favorite chicken recipes. In 1983, he started eating chicken—and hitting. He won the batting title that year. Boggs thought eating the chicken helped him. So he kept eating it. Eventually he earned the nickname "Chicken Man."

Boggs batting during a 1986 World Series game

NO SQUEAKY GEARS

Satchel Paige was both a Negro Leagues and MLB legend. For much of his career, MLB was **segregated**. Paige didn't join MLB until he was 42 years old. His arm still had plenty of life, though. He credited his success to a special **ointment**. He said he received it from the Sioux of North Dakota.

The ointment Paige used was said to be made with rattlesnake venom and gunpowder. Paige would rub it on his arm after every game, much to the horror of his teammates.

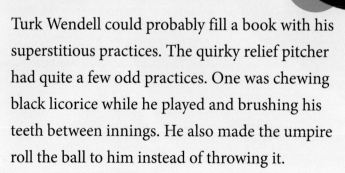

A MAJOR LEAGUE CHARACTER

Turk Wendell could probably fill a book with his superstitious practices. The quirky relief pitcher had quite a few odd practices. One was chewing black licorice while he played and brushing his teeth between innings. He also made the umpire roll the ball to him instead of throwing it.

Paige pitching for the Kansas City Athletics in 1965

CHAPTER 4

STADIUM FUN

Anything can happen during a baseball game. The action on the field is always exciting. And there are plenty of stadium traditions that add to the excitement.

OFF TO THE RACES

Where can you see giant meat products race each other? In Milwaukee. Watching the Famous Racing Sausages has become a tradition for Brewers fans. The hot dog, the Polish sausage, the Italian sausage, the chorizo, and the bratwurst battle during every game. The Famous Racing Sausages are so popular that several Brewers players have worn the costumes.

The Famous Racing Sausages compete during a 2008 Brewers game.

Mascot races are now a fan favorite for several MLB teams. The Presidents Race takes place in Washington, DC. And characters from the movie *Anchorman* race in San Diego.

SWIMMING SPECTATORS

At Arizona's Chase Field, there's a pool in the outfield where fans can gather. And every so often a home run splashes down in the water for a wet souvenir for a lucky fan.

BEAT THE FREEZE

In Atlanta, one lucky fan races against the Freeze, a superhero with blazing speed. The fan gets a head start, but it's still usually a long shot to win the race. A couple of lucky fans have beaten the Freeze. But the superhero is usually victorious.

THE FIRST PITCH

Right before a game starts, teams often have special guests throw a ceremonial first pitch. This practice started in 1910. President William Taft celebrated Opening Day by throwing the first pitch of the season.

Now teams invite all sorts of celebrities—from Olympic athletes to musicians to comedians—to throw out the first pitch. This has produced some awesome pitches and some hilariously bad tosses.

Olympian Simone Biles did an incredible flip before throwing her pitch at a 2019 World Series game. And rapper 50 Cent unleashed one of the wildest pitches of all time before a Mets game.

From wild first pitches to special songs to careful routines, teams and fans know how to make a baseball game lots of fun!

Simone Biles does a flip before throwing the first pitch of a 2019 World Series game.

GLOSSARY

bleachers (BLEE-chers)—seats organized like steps in a stadium

box score (BOKS SKOR)—a chart that shows plays during a baseball game

defiance (di-FAHY-uhns)—the act of challenging something

elaborate (i-LAB-ur-it)—complicated and detailed

fair (FAYRE)—inside the foul lines

feat (FEET)—an achievement that requires great courage, skill, or strength

foul (FOUL)—outside of the lines marking where a hit ball is fair

foul line (FOUL LINE)—lines on a baseball field showing fair and foul areas

jinx (JINKS)—to cause to have bad luck

long ball (LAWNG BAWL)—home run

ointment (OINT-muhnt)—a substance rubbed on one's skin to treat an injury, pain, or discomfort

ritual (RICH-oo-uhl)—an action that is always performed in the same way

rookie (RUK-ee)—a player who is playing their first year on a team

segregated (SEG-ruh-gay-ted)—separated by race

READ MORE

Burrell, Dean. *Baseball Biographies for Kids: The Greatest Players from the 1960s to Today.* Emeryville, CA: Rockridge Press, 2020.

Smith, Elliott. *Patience at the Plate: And Other Baseball Skills.* North Mankato, MN: Capstone, 2022.

Sturm, James. *Satchel Paige: Striking Out Jim Crow.* Los Angeles: Jump at the Sun / Disney Book Group, 2019.

INTERNET SITES

MLB Kids
mlb.com/fans/kids

Play Ball
playball.org

Sports Illustrated Kids: Baseball
sikids.com/baseball

INDEX

ABOUT THE AUTHOR

Elliott Smith is a freelance writer, editor, and author. He has covered a wide variety of subjects, including sports, entertainment, and travel, for newspapers, magazines, and websites. He has written a nonfiction book about the Washington Nationals and a children's book about Bryce Harper. He lives in the Washington, DC, area with his wife and two children.